I SPY
BIBLE
STICKER AND
ACTIVITY BOOK

This book belongs to

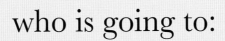

who is going to:

- read the Bible stories
- add the stickers
- do the puzzles and activities

Complete the pictures with stickers on every page

LION
CHILDREN'S

In the beginning

In the beginning, the Bible says,
God made the world and everything
in it.
"I'm pleased," said God.
"It's very, very good."

God made all the birds and the animals.
Can you guess what these animals are?

Find the stickers that
match the shape.

Spot and sticker

a peacock

the sun

a snake

Eve

three ducklings

a flamingo

Noah and the ark

God told Noah to build an ark.
  "Take your family on to the ark,"
said God, "and two of every kind
of animal.
"I will keep you safe from a flood. Then you
can start the world bright and new."

Noah took two of every kind of
animal on to the ark.

Can you match
the animal pairs?
Draw lines to
match them up.

Spot and sticker

two giraffes

two owls

two blue birds

two ostriches

Noah

Moses

God spoke to Moses.

"My people are sad, because they are slaves to a wicked king.

"I am choosing you to lead them to a land of their own.

"I will make a way through the sea so you can escape."

Spot and sticker

a mother and baby

a baby goat

a baby goat

a donkey

a fish

a starfish

a mother goat

Can you help Moses find his way across the sea?

David

Goliath was very tall
and very fierce.
He had a sword and a spear and a shield.
David was a shepherd boy.
He had a stick and a sling.
"God will help me beat you," said David.
He slung a stone.
Goliath fell down.

Spot and sticker

a butterfly

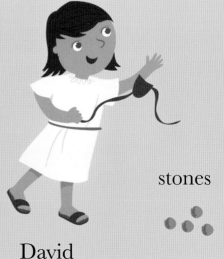

a sheep

a lizard

a vulture

David

stones

| START 1 | 2 | A downhill road. Have another go. 3 | 4 A soldier points the way. Go on 2. | 5 |

Use buttons and a dice to play the game and help David to reach Goliath.

		6
9 Ask God to help you. Go on 1.	8	7 Stop to pick up stones. Miss a go.
10		
11 Take deep breaths. Wait for a 3.	12	13 God helps you. Go on 3.
20 Ready to face Goliath!	19		14 An uphill road. Miss a go.

FINISH

| 18 Dropped a stone. Wait for a 2. | 17 See Goliath. Go on 2. | 16 | 15 |

Daniel

Daniel was in a deep, dark den. He was being punished by the emperor for saying his prayers.

God sent an angel into the den. The lions fell asleep.

God kept Daniel safe.

The emperor was amazed when he found Daniel sitting happily with the lions.

Who did God send to keep Daniel safe? Complete the dot-to-dot to find out.

Spot and sticker

 a lion cub

a pile of bones

 a spider

the emperor

 three rats

Daniel

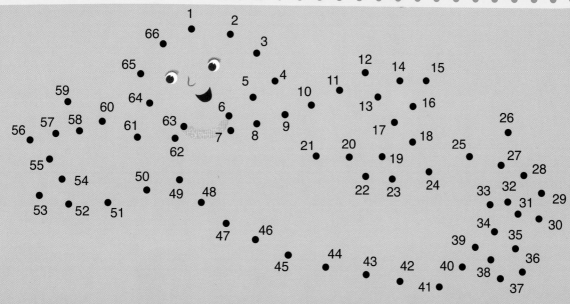

Baby Jesus

Here is the stable in Bethlehem.
Here are Joseph and Mary and little
baby Jesus.
Who else has come to see the baby?

Use stickers to complete the stable picture.
Who do you think was there with baby Jesus?

Wise men came to see baby Jesus as well.
Complete the dot-to-dot to find out what gifts
they gave him.

In the beginning

Noah

Moses

David

Daniel

Galilee

Easter garden

Baby Jesus

Lost sheep

Great feast

Jerusalem

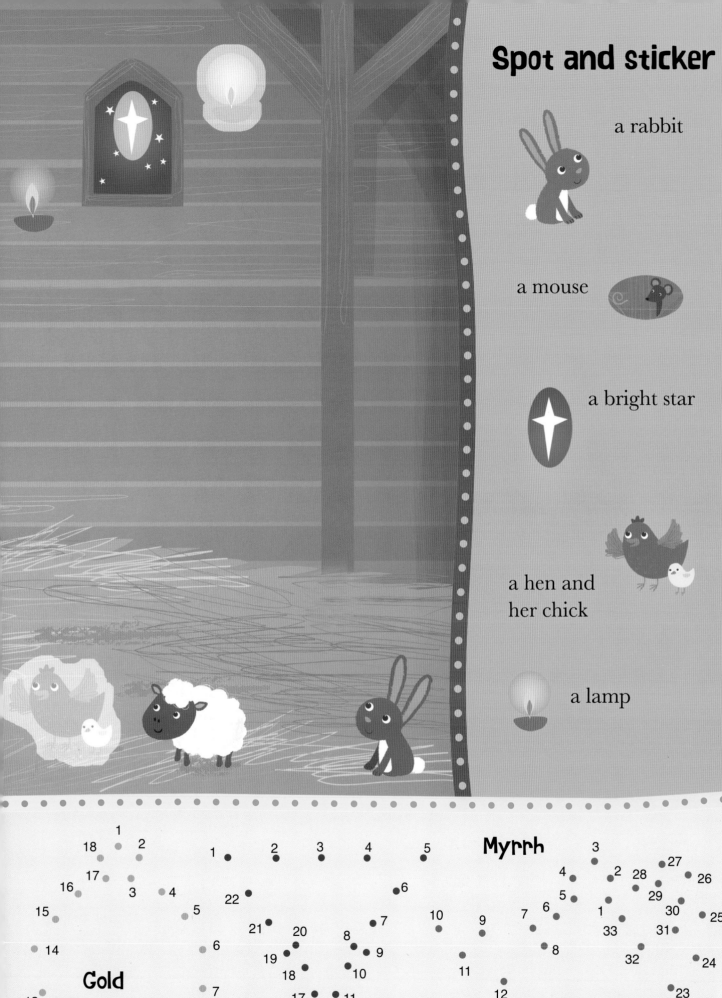

Spot and sticker

a rabbit

a mouse

a bright star

a hen and
her chick

a lamp

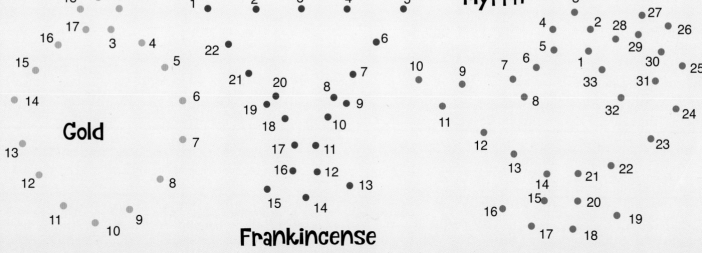

Gold

1
18   2
17   3   4
16
15
14   5   6   7   8
13
12   9 10 11

Frankincense

1   2   3   4   5
22   6
21   20   7   10
19   8   9
18   10
17   11
16   12   13
15   14

Myrrh

9   7   6   5   4   3
8   1   2   28   27   26
33   29   30   25
32   31   24
11   12   13   23
14   15   16   17   18   19   20   21   22

Jesus in Galilee

On the hills of Galilee, Jesus was talking. "Love one another," he said. "Forgive one another. Then you will be God's children. God will always take care of you."

Jesus said that God will take care of us, just like he takes care of the birds and the flowers.

Make these pretty flowers like the ones Jesus spoke about.

1 For each flower head, draw around a glass to get a circle about 5cm across. Add stickers or decorations.

 a goat

a boat

 a sheep

a boy with
a basket

 Jesus

a cat

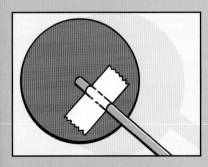

2 Paint flower sticks or
drinking straws green,
and tape onto the back of
the flower.

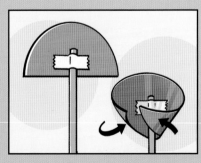

3 For each bud, cut a circle
piece in half. Tape onto
a flower stick and fold as
shown.

Jesus' story of the lost sheep

The shepherd had spent all day looking for his lost sheep. He got home at sunset.

He called to his friends. "I found my lost sheep," he said. "Let's have a party."

God is like that shepherd, and God is happy when someone who was lost is found.

Spot and sticker

a snake

a sheep

a jackal

a wolf

the good shepherd

Can you help the shepherd find which path leads to his lost sheep?

Jesus' story of the great feast

A rich man was giving a party.
   The people he had invited didn't turn up.
   He sent his servant to invite poor people. They came at once and were happy.

Can you spot the difference between these two feasts?

a cat

a boy with a crutch

a fish dish

a young girl drinking

the rich man

There are 8 to find.

Riding to Jerusalem

Jesus was riding to the big city of Jerusalem.
People cheered and waved palm leaves.
"We want you to be our king!" they cried.
But Jesus had enemies. They frowned.

After arriving in Jerusalem, Jesus had a meal with his friends. They ate special bread and Jesus asked them to always remember him.

Ask an adult to help you make your own special bread.

1 Measure 150g wholemeal flour and 1 teaspoon of salt into a bowl. Add 2 tablespoons of olive oil, then add water, little by little, to make a stiff dough.

Spot and sticker

a girl waving a palm leaf

palm leaves

a girl playing a musical pipe

a Pharisee

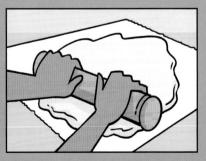

2 Lay a piece of baking parchment on a worktop and use a rolling pin to roll the dough very thin. Lift onto a baking tray.

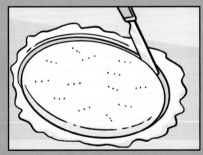

3 Cut out a big circle. Prick all over with a fork.

4 Bake for 15–17 minutes until crisp and just turning brown. Remove from the oven to cool slightly and turn the oven off.

The Easter garden

The frowning people had Jesus killed.
His body was in a tomb.
  His friends went to say a last goodbye.
  They saw angels in the tomb.
  "Jesus isn't here," the angels said.
"God has made him alive again."

Mary and many of Jesus' friends saw him
alive again and they told everybody about
the miracle.

Can you help Mary to find Jesus?

a dove

a rabbit

Mary
Magdalene

a sheep

an angel

a bird's
nest

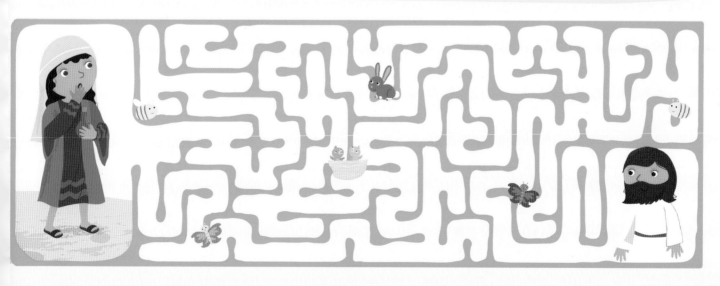

Answers